FISH COLORING BOOK FOR KIDS

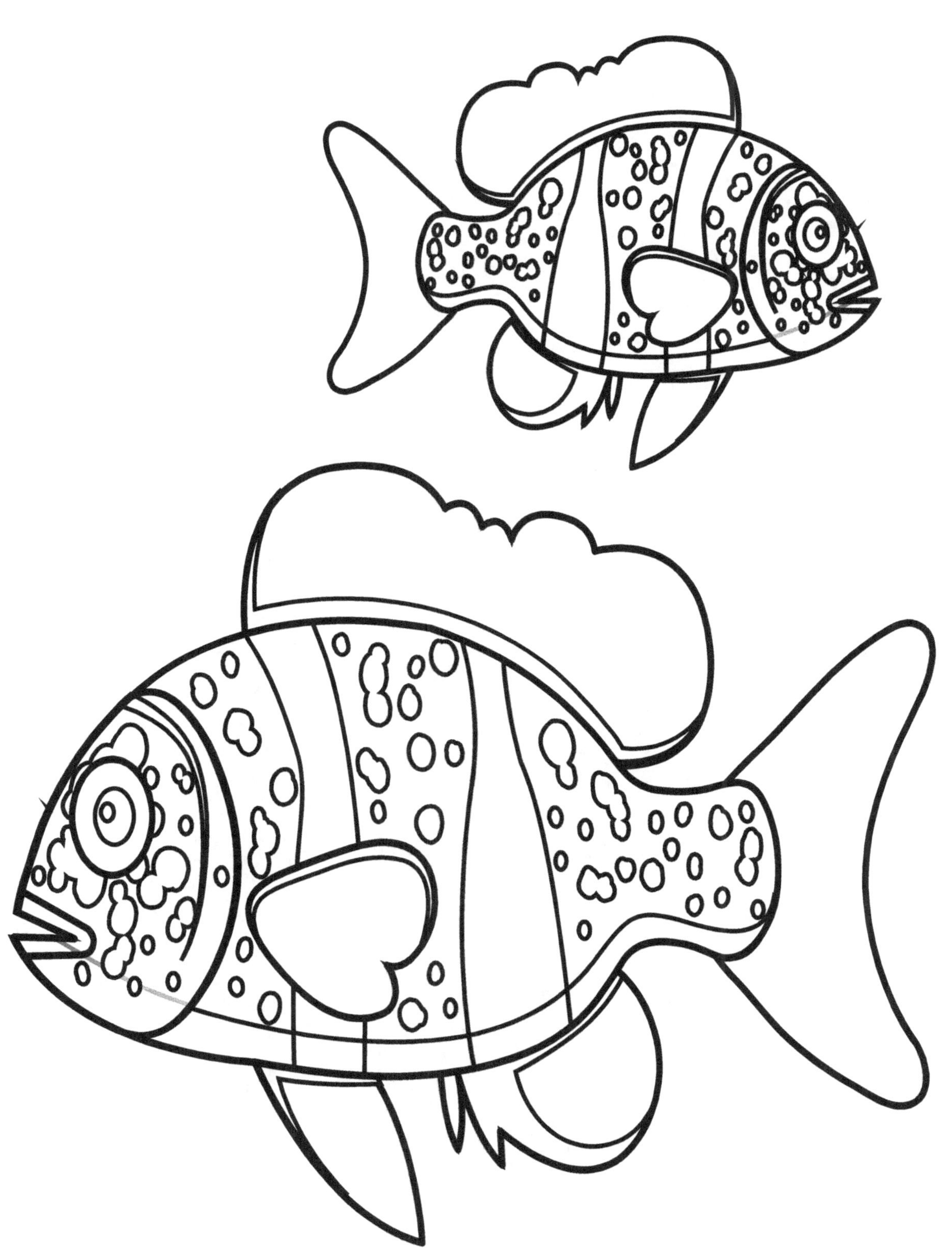

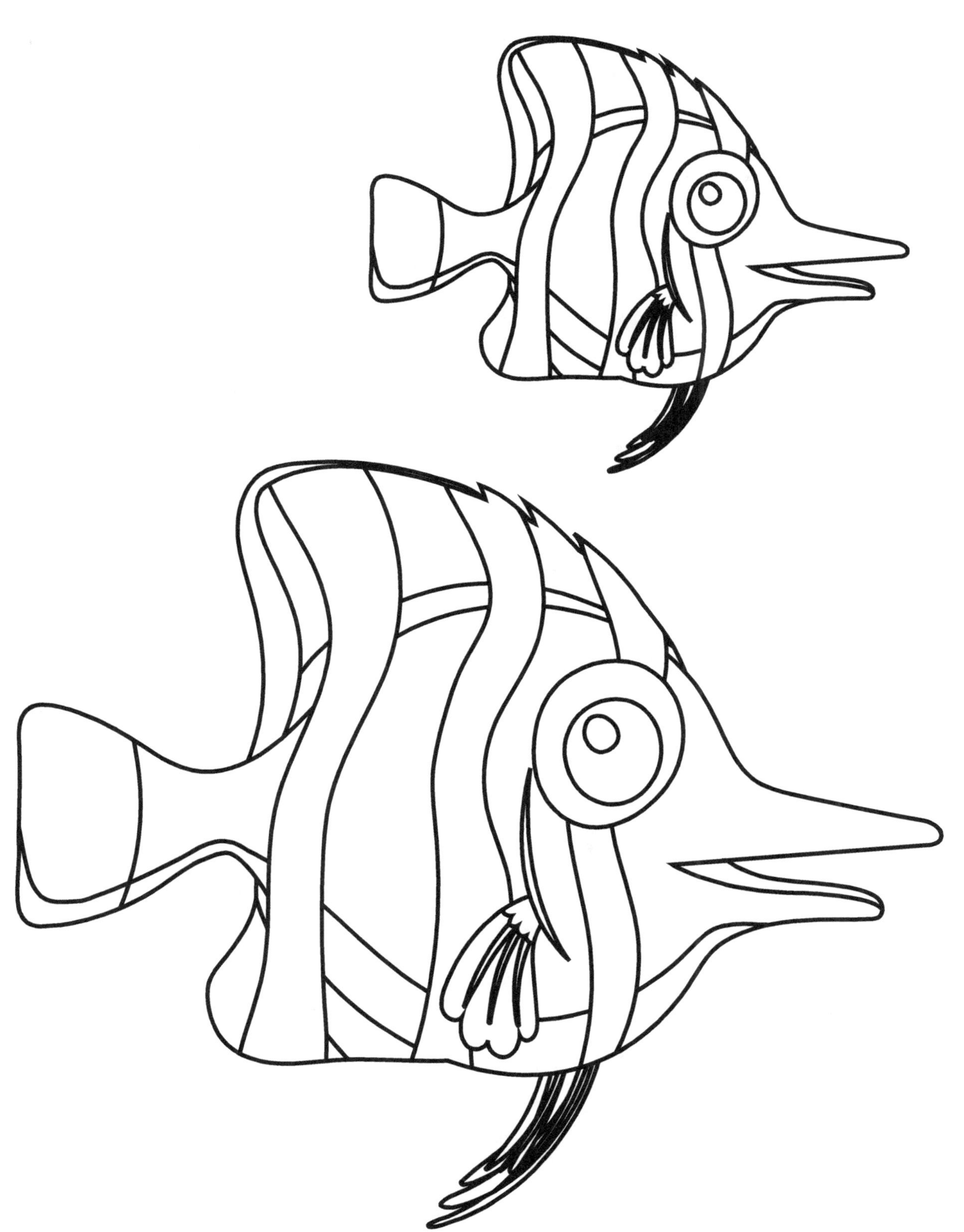

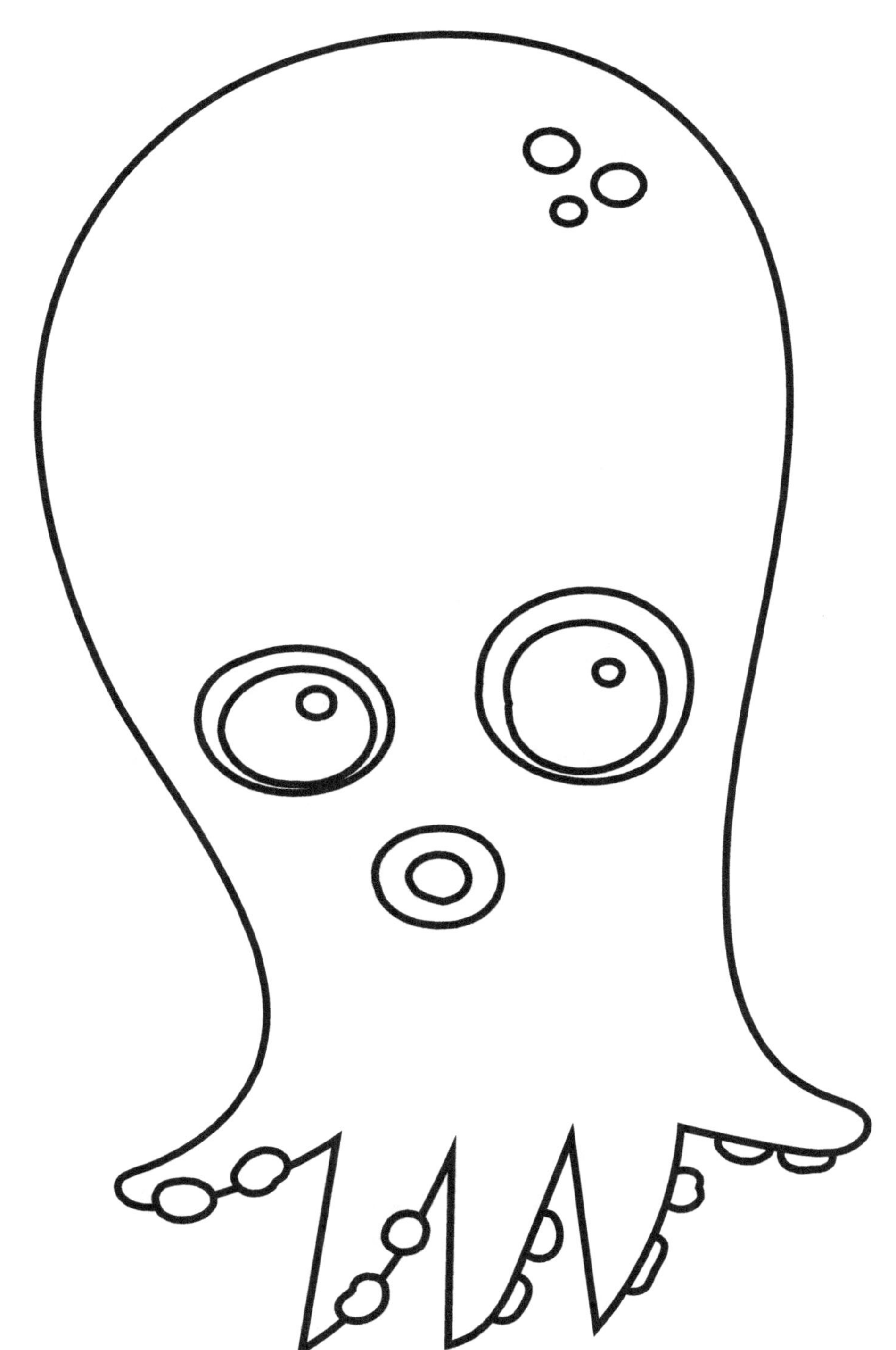

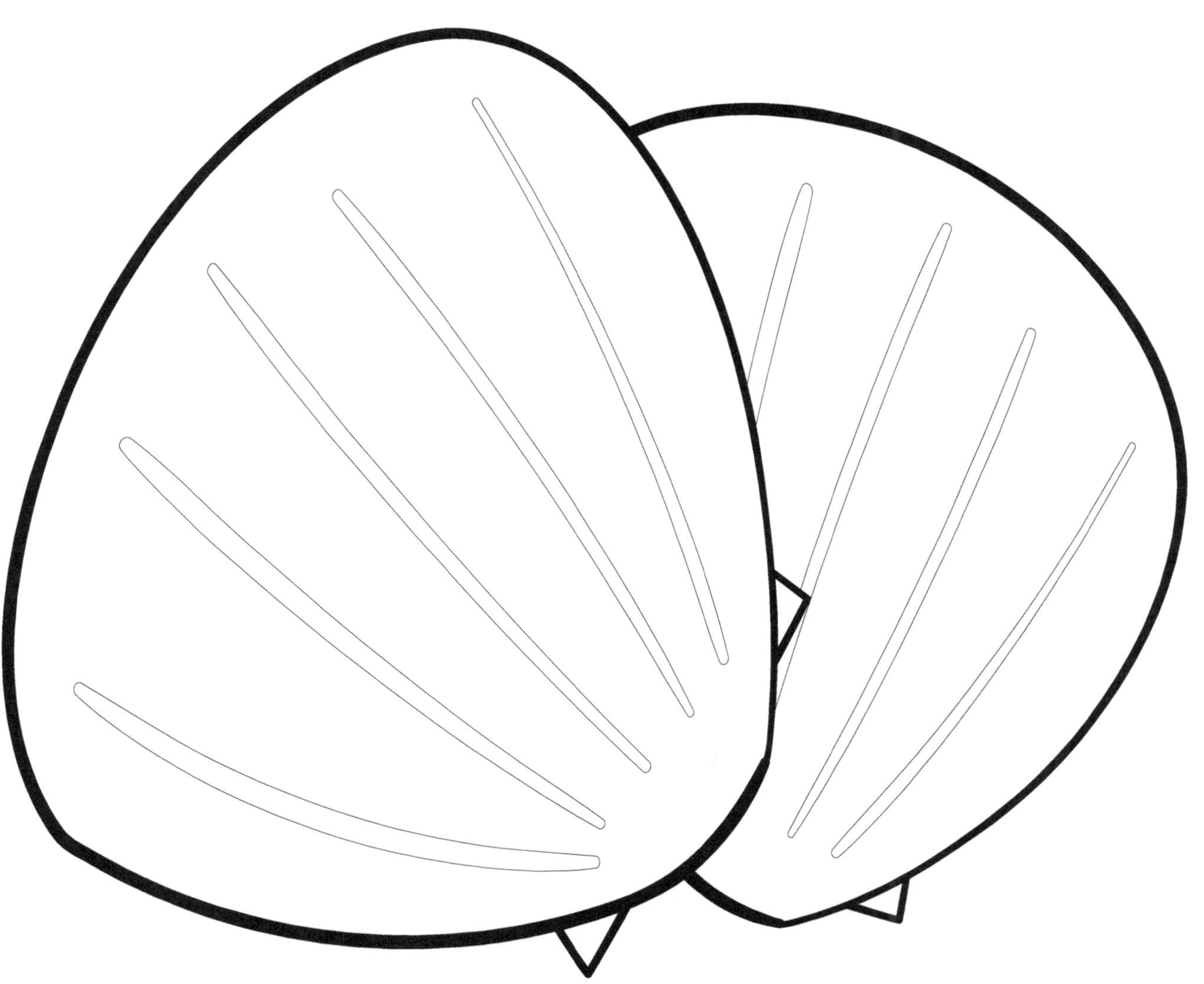

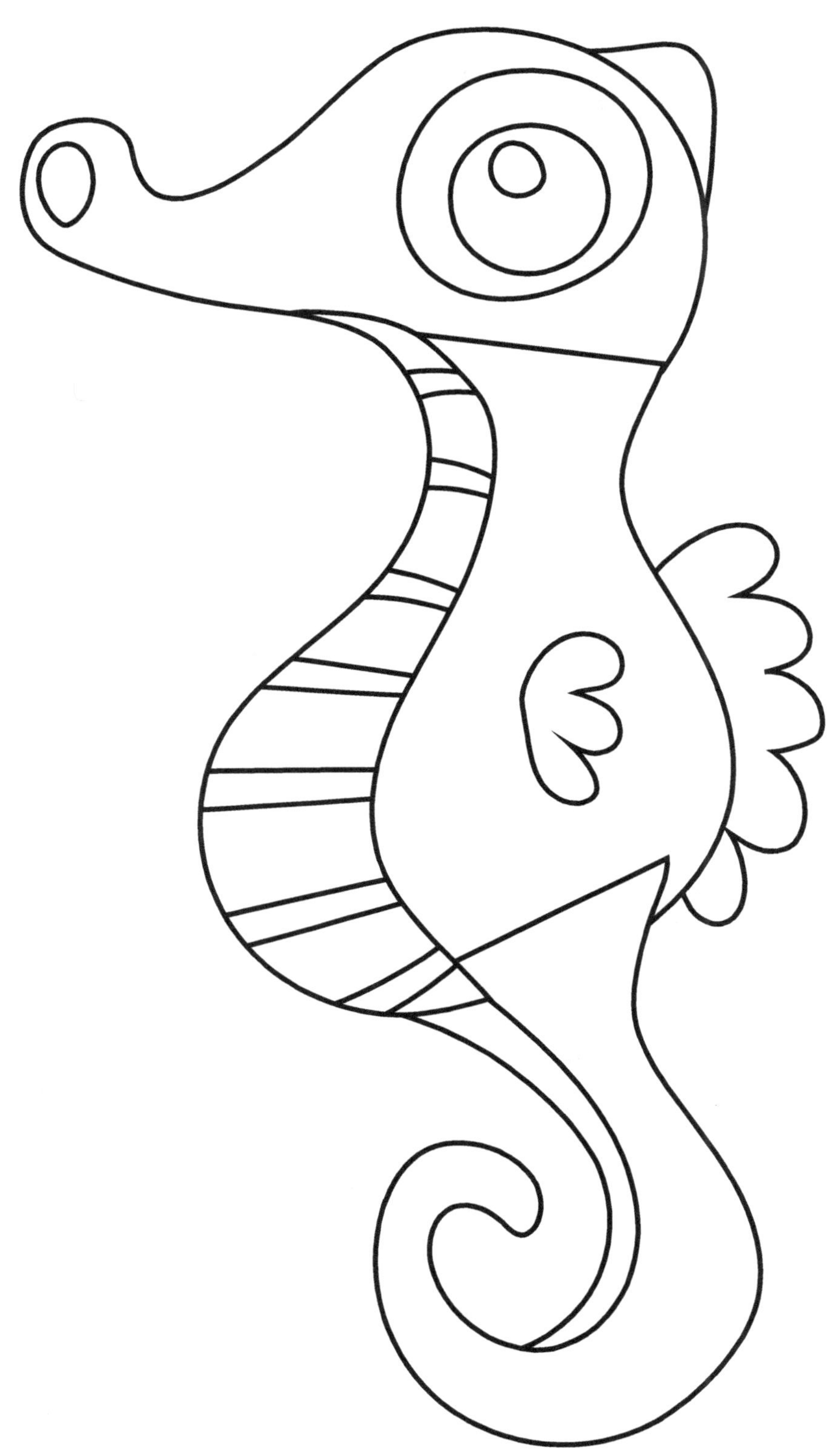

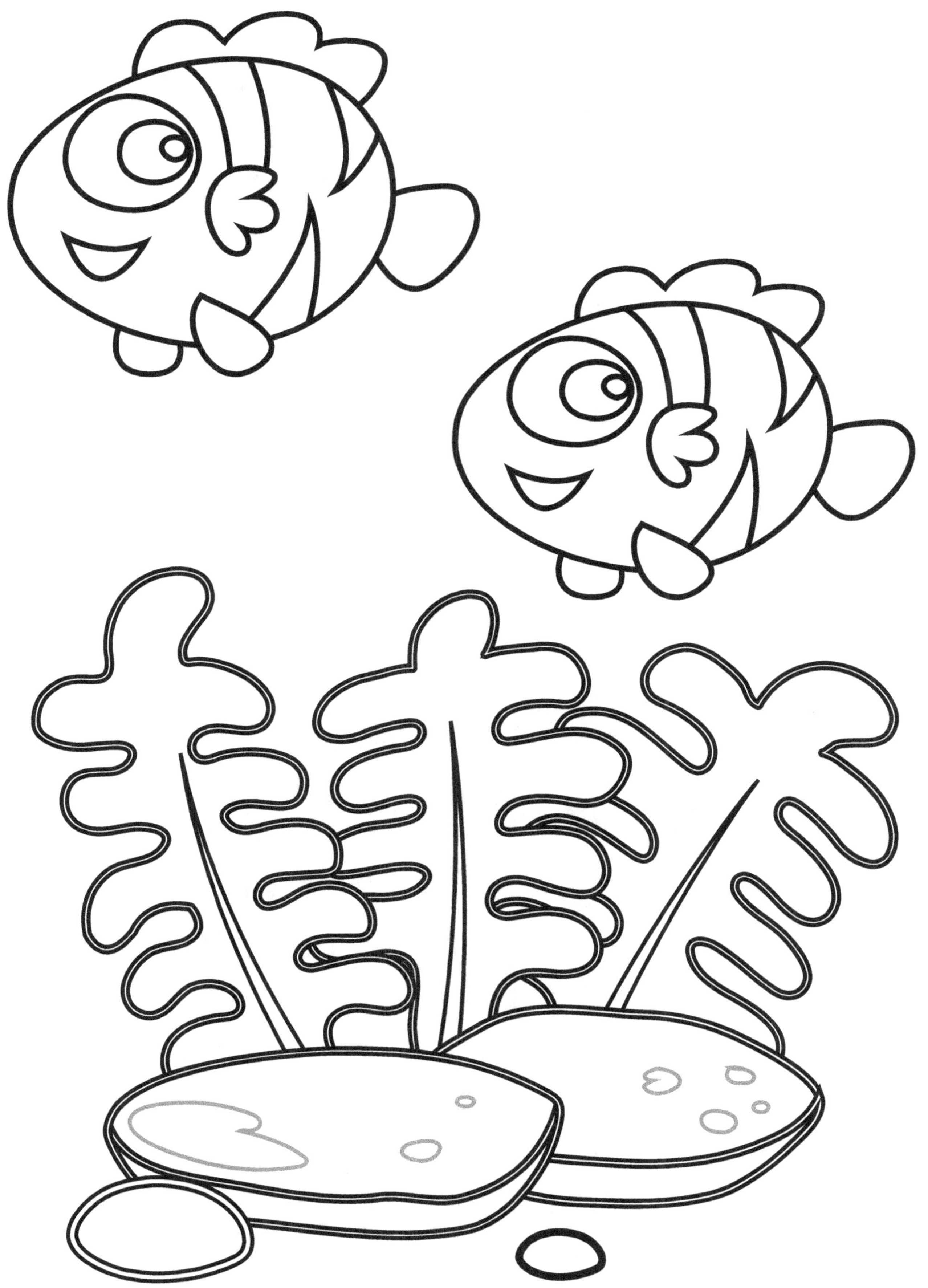